POLYCHROMASIA

POLYCHROMASIA

Mohineet Kaur Boparai

MAWENZI
HOUSE

We acknowledge the support of the Canada Council for the Arts for our publishing program. We also acknowledge support from the Government of Ontario through the Ontario Arts Council.

Cover design by Sabrina Pignataro
Cover photo: Vizerskaya / Colors exploding stock photo / iStockphoto.com

Library and Archives Canada Cataloguing in Publication

Title: Polychromasia / Mohineet Kaur Boparai.
Names: Boparai, Mohineet Kaur, 1985- author.
Description: Poems.
Identifiers: Canadiana (print) 2019019023X | Canadiana (ebook) 20190190248 | ISBN 9781988449937 (softcover) | ISBN 9781988449944 (HTML) | ISBN 9781988449951 (PDF)
Classification: LCC PR9499.4.B67 P65 2019 | DDC 821/.92—dc23

Printed and bound in Canada by Coach House Printing

Mawenzi House Publishers Ltd.
39 Woburn Avenue (B)
Toronto, Ontario M5M 1K5
Canada
www.mawenzihouse.com

For My Son, Himmat
I picked you up and wrote you in my breath
Not like a kite but a dandelion feather, this
Sting at its base looking for a page

CONTENTS

Introduction   *ix*

Proem   *1*
The Muse as Hanuman   *2*
Tribal Prayer   *4*
Eight Love Poems for Guramrit   *5*
Distance   *8*
Our Conversation   *9*
When You Come in the Night   *11*
Moments in Moga   *12*
Candle   *13*
The First Thought of You   *14*
Feeding   *15*
First Born   *17*
Morning Prayer   *19*
Storytelling   *21*
The Star Within   *23*
Sati   *24*
On a Photograph in a Social Studies Textbook   *25*
Anthophilous   *27*
Art Workshop in a Slum   *28*
On a Map Reading   *29*
A Poet on Baisakhi, 1919   *30*
The Splitting   *31*
For My Grandfather   *32*
Artist   *33*
Not Every Poem   *34*
A Day with Keats   *35*
A Van Gogh Tale   *37*

I Like That Kind of Home   39
A Butterfly Sees   40
Sea Otter   41
Fire   42
Extra Terrestrial   43
Room   45
Sinking   47
Evolution   48
Repression   49
Neurotic   50
Normal or Abnormal   51
Sethe   52
Fables   54
Sleeping Beauty   55
Beauty and the Beast   56
On Death   58
Raj. Mala. Heer.   59
Conversation of Continents   61
Some Ekphrastic Poems   63
Bloom   65
Mother   66
Lilies in the Grave   67
Haikus   69
A Tree's Polychromasia   71
Before Nirvana   72
Morning   74

Acknowledgements   77

Introduction

"Polychromasia," the word, literally refers to multiplicity of colours; in medical terminology, however, it is a condition where immature red blood cells are found in the blood stream, having been released prematurely by the bone marrow. The title of this book suggests that the poetry in it explores, metaphorically, the multiple colours of people, places, situations and objects and at the same time attempts to reach into what is ailing, abnormal, or dysfunctional. In this book I explore the vague spaces of life that are raw, being not yet inscribed with human existence. It will also be explored how these spaces, when lived in, become places with specific meanings to human life. This concept is explored particularly within the demographical space of India, more so with respect to the more elaborate landscape of existence where the elements, environment, and human life intersect. The interplay of nature and culture is explored, as is the functioning of a binary world and the effect of such divisions on the human psyche.

This book, I feel, was impending because my poetry in general is encrusted in colour and it is for me a way of relating to the world. My poems are initiated as recordings of the nuances of sensory experience, and some form of philosophical understanding then ensues. The images come first and then the idea takes root.

Colour is central to the exposition of experience in my poetry, in which truths become interlinked with colour. The poetry in this volume is already foreshadowed in my previous work. I write in my introduction to *The Wind in a Seashell* (2016), "This book's poetry is a chameleon of sorts—a multi-pigmented being, a cold hibernating organism, clinging to wood and leaf till it is itself no more and changes—a geo-morph and climato-morph. Biology and geography come synced through paint and pigment." In the present volume I aim at locating the life colours of different objects and situations. Everything has a colour or colours that emerge in our perception as we go about understanding it. Painters understand this well, especially the surrealists and expressionists. Colours for the lay person are often associated with race, cultural objects, emotions, the environment, weather, health, atmosphere, diagnoses of diseases, etc. and therefore connote what one experiences in some form or another.

The late Dr P Ranchan, on reading my first book, advised me that my poetry lacked muscle. I grappled with understanding his words as an amateur poet and then understood that my poems then were primarily perceptive, rooted in objects and experiences of them. They lacked muscle because perhaps they were a bit too closely concerned with a newly turned adult's individualism and how the objects around her looked in the spotty sunshine of the individual she was, in the process of discovering. Perception is still very much an aspect of the poetry in this collection too, and the poems take a route inwards from what begins in the eye, but are more universally nuanced and less starkly individualistic as compared to the earlier poems. I become a medium and not the substance of these verses. There has been some form of enlargement of the process of seeing. These poems are denser than those in my first collection. Some form of experiment of writing that started then, however, continues; experiment is an endless process in the artist's life.

The poetic journey at some point has to go through a looking inwards. The process of seeing in poetry involves love and the heart, which are so spontaneously and naturally engaged that they become silent forces. Voice has to lean to it like it has to be to all other seen objects. What is within and what is outside are both important. One cannot overestimate the importance of heart to poetry. Detachment of the writing process may seem like a noble road, but it is also a road obscured because of the half-hearted involvement of the poet with life. And so this volume begins with some love poems.

Poetry involves observation of oneself, the outer world and something extraperceptive and therefore unnamable. One realizes in the process of observation that there are certain qualities of inanimate things and creatures that define them. There are at the same time certain qualities that are universal. A mature poet balances the universal and personal in her poetry.

There are poems which try to understand the various systems that we humans find ourselves parts of, including the biosphere and environment, the patriarchal system, class system, and other ways of classifying people. For example, the poems relating to the biosphere are expressions about geographical space, its characteristics of nurture and threat, and how humans have related to this space over history. The idea is to explore the multiple phases and aspects of human relationship with this system. Other poems take the reader not to the outside world, but within the human inner space.

Dark spaces open up in the poems that involve the human psyche. These dark spaces have gravity or they are endless and light, space leading to space, or yet again, they are heavy. This darkness, however, is not without colour, as the poem "Lilies in a Grave—A Brain Scan" unveils:

> I have somewhere a dried lily in the head.
> I wish upon the scan,
> the buckled ball of snow
> daubed with orange and green,
> I look closely, and there is yellow and blue too.

And then this shower of hail in my skull
the bruises—flowers shedding pigment,
ice lodged in cerebral cavities—

drooping on a summer stem
there is a hot fruit of fire.
Lucifer flocking souls in his bag
of snakes, the venom sweet
but they writhe through my nerves.
Forget the codeword and you are lost.

In another poem, "Sati," which is a feminist poem, darkness comes through light. "Sati" was a practice in India that lasted until the nineteenth century, in which a widow was burnt on her husband's pyre, ironically to save her from a disgraceful life henceforth. The poem goes:

I stumble over their stringent promise of death
this pyre, a casement
of perfume they dip me in.
How it sticks to my lips.
And death's ligament peels in places
when they plug it with fire.
I'm already a turnip,
how I melt into the air.
My shrieks
forced out of a thorny throat.
This is how I take flight—through
the blisters of my final roast.

Darkness holds the energy to bring forth light into existence as in the Big Bang or in meditation. The poem "Sleeping Beauty" is about the light that comes from darkness. It understands Buddha's life through the metonymous fairy tale:

This is time come to a standstill.
How long will the sands pour in the hour glass?
This single prick is hard enough to
send Buddha into convulsions
it takes exactly one hundred revolutions
for the kiss to compel life
then the clocks begin again
the bustle resumes
and Buddha awakes;
with the kiss of eternity on his lips
this betrothal is juice

Another major theme in this collection is change. Change is inevitable, but humans need some form of stability too. Often humans turn to tradition to seek answers to present concerns. The poem "Tribal Prayer" concludes with an answer to a fast-paced life:

he whispers, there is green in the dark
always paisleys hide in black mango boughs.
If you are attentive, you can smell flowers
inside every fruit. If you peel it right
sometimes the petals will touch your fingertips.

But you must be really slow
and when you bite
the mouth dries and you consume
the remnants of God's dusky morning.

As a poet I have come to the understanding that things fit, even when it seems otherwise. Everything has a shape that is contained by space, or it displaces something in space. A major theme in several poems is that of containment, whether it is within a physical space such as a room, or is socially generated through custom, or is within a historical context.

The poetry in this book tries to discover and disclose certain truths. Truths are subjective and localized and "the Truth" exists beyond space and time and hence is elusive. The truths of a poet while writing are more intricate and multifaceted than the truths she carries with her in routine life. This is because the truth of poetry is intrinsic and deep-seated. When poets seem to be having out-of-body experiences during writing, it is because certain hidden parts of their selves are being divulged in the process. They are, while writing, unlike their normal selves. Discovery of the truth comes through the writing and not before it. When I read what I have written, I understand it from several viewpoints that have unconsciously found a way into the poem.

Every author breathes the spaces that he or she inhabits. Their perspectives are moulded by the environmental, psychological, and cultural spaces within which they exist. The author, as it were, contracts this vastness into a microcosm in her mind that in turn is conveyed in her writing (this is, incidentally, how all human understanding of the universe operates—through a contraction of it), through words, images, sound, rhythm, etc. during the creative writing process. Their collaboration on the page resonates then within the author's mind and on the page.

-MKB
January, 2018

Proem

God sends truth like bubble rain
bursting through a photograph
each, rainbow-studded, clear, brittle

or the orgasm between my legs,
slow surge,
spreading over my soul like a shroud
this one that leaves me dead
for just a moment.

Just a book flipping in the wind
with words that you can only feel
with an invisible finger.
Old nails grow from it extending to the sun
like flames rising from earth.
This one made from termite-eaten pages.

It is a cube fitting a sphere
It is coloured black
It is the rainbow of a bruise
The spectrum that flows outward from the head.
But almost always, a halo contains
almost always, in this one glass bubble of fire
your promise to the body has to shatter.

The Muse as Hanuman[1]

There, on the shallow ocean,
you will find a bridge,
made by an army of monkeys,
led by an ancient god.
Some place, I think, I saw him
bathing in mud,
nothing like an angry bull,
but a rainbow rising to the clouds.
He knows the sky's juice and the earthy pollen touch
and the flower of fire that envelops.
When he lit Lanka with
the flame bud on his tail
his godly backbone grew a vertebra.

I was told once, he creeps up
from a corner of your dreamland
and sits under the tree brushing
immensity against your window.
Then, in the shadow of the winnowing
curtain he disappears and stray leaves settle
around your four-post casket.
Sometimes in the street you see a shady palm
and in a hot day's glance something vanishes
around the corner with a tail.

The sky above his translucent face unpeeling
like butter-paper onions
and the dazed eyes open under a cover.

---

1   Hanuman, a devotee of Lord Rama, is one of the main characters in
Ramayana, and is also mentioned in several other religious texts like the
Mahabharata. Also known as the son of Wind, he is physically very strong.
He is considered to have been a disciple of the Sun-god and hence very
knowledgeable.

He chants, "I can read eyes like a human
I boast the spells I cast with my hands
I can write the jungle down in twigs
I can hear it growling in my ears."

He writes draining a shadowy ink,
this blue shade alighting on the windy page.
He is my sentence-maker,
the one who destroys knowledge
as he swallows the sun.
The celibate words cry out a poem
this coalescing of seas in my womb,
they collect sand from the deltaic fingers
of rivers lurking in his shade,
unburdened by manliness.
Celibacy of the pen is fortitude
the son of the wind is in my womb
singing through his broken jaw.

Tribal Prayer

At night God always knocks.
Sometimes he comes as a jasmine bough
enjoying his scent,
through the cup of
flower opening to the wind.

Then sometimes he has a
maroon face and snowy head
he talks through the night's quiet
he sleeps in my house and the
windows he climbed through, pay obeisance.

Or he comes in sleepless nights
riding a flood, the land shaky underfoot
flushed air falls into our souls
winnowing tree and land.
He is angry, we accept.

He cleanses, we open ourselves
like lattice doors
his breath blows through us
as we await his jasmine,
we let his light pass through
he whispers, there is green in the dark
always paisleys hide in black mango boughs.
If you are attentive, you can smell flowers
inside every fruit. If you peel it right
sometimes the petals will touch your fingertips.

But you must be really slow
and when you bite
the mouth dries and you consume
the remnants of God's dusky morning.

Eight Love Poems for Guramrit

Sealed

Can you hear my breath,
and the hiss between my tongue and lip?
A downy pit of a fruit lodges my voice.
It knocks its stiff knuckles
on this door from yesteryear.
Just before I suffocate,
and just as it becomes a drone,
you open this sealed door
and a whale sails away
with its feather fountain
on the whiffs of the ocean's gulp.

You Calm My Storm

You calm my storm, the red of my fever
and something falls through
the whirlpool of the sky, dragging sound, leaving succour.
My hands are fresh from your perfume
it is the whiff of the Jupiter sky
with sixteen moons to cover up the universe.
The pink dust of an asteroid storm
lies in wait; their molten cores
have not yet dried.
They contain perfect spheres
in their universal memory
and you tranquilize me in their perfection.

The purple Aurora Borealis falls flat on the sky,
angry like an empty stomach.
You smoothen with your cool breath,
the green smear of this light you contain,
and in the blue black bruise that
the sky has become,
you are Venus on a frozen chariot.
All the time, our supple promise stays folded
between your sky and mine,
and between the two palms of your quietness

The First Day We Met

Leaves floated out like little
oyster shells
opening golden sun breaths
under oceanic boughs,
the throaty trees were still
and their share of green became
gills fluttering with every pulse.
When you looked up,
the moment confessed itself
the white whales we had floated
across the Indian ocean, warm
they leapt like tigers through
the burning ring of the Equator.
The smell of spring was sour
its gulps of air filled us
this, we will remember.
The moment seems quiet
like a ray floating dust.
Yesterday I smelt the Walkman case
from that day, to uncover

the dusty layer of perfume
and I inhaled it again.
The perfume was gone,
the soul was still unfurling in its vapours.

Distance

Mid-flight we met, torn in places
torn in each other and encased in our storms,
later, we are fluffy like straw pillows—
resting our heads on the earth
sweaty as ice cubes, flushed like the sun
stagnant as mud,
we try to remember beyond the journey.

The rainy tread is slippery
above in the sky, the
grazing jaws of light are dry.
Far, far away, in a grassland, marsupials jump
with joeys in their pockets
as far as Australia, I thought at first,
as far as that winding.
But the days now lose count.

This is a blue-green tale that
I see in the colours of a hot spring
but the glass of God's eyes is stone dead
nothing flickers beyond the big bang.

The heavy promise of the day
will expand like watercolour in a drop,
the slow curtain will fall
but the light is blinding
the promise is heavy
and God is silent.

Our Conversation

(About my first letter to Amrit)

Again I gave you the plum squish and
a honey-dipped sun
you swallowed the lull of my chords.
Every night the howl of wolves,
the tripping doe with magic antlers,
the hop and croak of grey frogs
startled the yolk of love.

I wrote you that letter,
with an alphabet from our each day together.
It travelled far like the strongest sperms
written in the blue of the moonlit
night sky, it was red where the sky
ended in a throat,

when the song ended, I breathed again
I hung your music
to dry on my bones
you urged the patchy dawn to
compliance, and it froze
you canvassed the sun with a sail
and it folded in its shadows.

It was not pillow talk, these conversations,
they were tiny droplets of a drizzle,
I sang to the trailing current
I sang with the squish of grass under sodden feet,
from dew-lined neck with a juicy core.
The smell was everywhere, where you
had frayed that first letter in the hot spell

of your anxiety to meet me.
The fever of your touch was tranquilizing
your hands are like the dance of
an araucaria in the wind
your voice, a dark cave with
tiger eyes nudging the last light.
The delirious sun draws a line
on the horizon and we write.

When You Come in the Night

I spent last night in the strokes of the story you told me.
Every time the clock struck an hour and you still spoke
the grassland of my desire blew in the wind
and at midnight, a primrose
blossomed lonely in the garden.

When the flit of feathers ruffled in my wind,
your shade over me
had already lengthened with the betraying dials
under the moonlight.
I woke to the pressure of the night's
fingers on my nape
I threaded my way through its fabric
and there
between the stars
and the lunatic moon, you
were the yarn, sewing the sky together.
You walked from the mystical moon
and prised the sun's panorama from a peg.

You spread through the blue of the sky.
You curl up the clouds of my breath
close to your chest
you know the colours of my chameleon skin—
the shades of my visage,
the stiff promise of my letters,
the unspooling of my dreaming nights.
And when you arrive,
in the night,
I cling to you, smothered
between the sun and the moon like a kiss.

Moments in Moga

This was before I knew you belonged there,
before the four corners of your garden
unloaded their fluffy scent along my paths.
I shuffle up my head to find you
for the first time in this once
forgotten city. That was
before the fire pressed me
like a flower between
layers of you.

Who knew this dried flower
would float this distance?
But it bloomed sunlight,
the sky, glazed, shone.
It was a promise like an oversize
world map, too difficult to unfold.

I—a particle—have landed in its effable dust,
but now the faces on its roads are a haze.
The dream's cake already savoured
I cannot pull cherries from its cream pegs,
but its weight in my abdomen
lines it silver and
a cloud rises from it.
The cradle that rocked me through
this town two decades ago is already still,
the pulse in my wrist
seethes with fire
it comes and goes,
but will always return
because I am here again,
this time, to stay.

Candle

This candle aligned on a nautical elbow
swims slowly at sea
and these waxen sea chariots are
drawn by the breaths of a shy sea creature.
Crimson is the hand of this wick
not dimmed to ash, it holds this flame
that extends skywards.
Always the itch of fire in its bones.
But this is a stir she consumes
the wax melts into a pool
the thread catches our talk
it twists around itself but never are
the words shed, never is it wrung dry.

You cull out silences like a great artist
or like this stem of a candle
I muster up words from a serpent lair.
Like a wick, draped in you
together, the silence and hiss rejoice
while the light burns on. It burns in our eyes
never too early to close
never too early to sleep,
awake as a flame in a temple.

The First Thought of You

For my son, Himmat

That day in Phuket, the sea
became the colour of my veins
and the salmon sky was persimmon pulp.
A pair of seagulls swayed in the air
and the wind twitched
around our faces, smudged
in a curious light.
The growl of an animal lingered
between a pair of solitary swimmers,
and that anchored ship.
I imagined them, newly met, lost
to us, rapt in their first stir.

You were already
splashing inside me
a love song had already
left my follicles.
Later, when a hasty bus
bumped you into me, I said
the first loud prayer for you,
I had rehearsed it in my teenage mind
I had already placed teddies on your cot
heard the softness of my lullabies.
How young were my thoughts then,
but I grow with you.
The first thought of you was
like this sea that I could not hold
in my palms. This surge is slow
the surf is pure salt
with a promise that does not dry up.

Feeding

For my son, Himmat

Before you cry, my milk
already drips,
the lemon t-shirt blots away
this salubrious nectar
stiff roots dry up in the t-shirt's piquant sheet

like your mind's atoms
moving between your mind and mine,
before you dig into me your bald gums
you are already there in my heartbeat
you linger in the hollow basket, talking
to cherry tendrils and coral sinews.
You are a night creature still, and this kick in me
resonates with the moonlight.

Every burst of breath is still
before it reaches you,
you have touched
the strength of my muscles
smelt every tissue in anticipation.
The supple floating womb
and the breath of life, you hold
for nine months as you dive,
the unborn yogi,
is not my making
I am no Michelangelo.

As the milk fills you,
outside the window,
a coal myna sings to the cow.

It is not alone
the tussle of araucaria calls
for it to come, the gum oozing out of the bark
whispers to the wind its welcome
the winsome air is alive
its gusts beat like your heart
and with the surge of my milk
I realize, there are other sounds
besides my heartbeat
that you have heard,
and other music besides my
dreams will enthrall you.

First Born

For my son, Himmat

Slow like a season, you come.
We have cradled you in our breaths
our hands already like sails grappling with
the gusting winds that blow past your ship.

The slush of rain in my womb
its pitter-patter lulls you to sleep
the torches show you my pigment, you move,
before you stretch out of me like a sun beam.

My soul reflected on a blank wall shudders for you
and the prisms of my eyes float rainbows.
Every now and then a thought of fear falls
and slumps into the mind.

We shed these skins as we slither out of stones and cracks
your mouth opens, a quiet tinkle fermenting sound,
your voice joins this space between us—new parents—
the lingering cloud between us squeezed like a lemon.

The universe is a slow
clumsy knife in a desert. Its blank perils,
its frowns in the tropical foliage, its nebulous nails,
scratching for you, illusions curl in my head's desert.

No more am I a sack spilling seeds.
I feel roots growing from my toes,
my stem has a waxen promise that transpires
leaf after shady leaf, speaks in whiffs to you.

This begins, not from your vowels, but before;
it was already thumping, before the water
sewed itself to the sky and the rains never stop
floating boats in my veins.

This is not like the heavy air in a chamber
or the burdened seed that splits.
It is a transformation of the elements:
I snuggle up this scent—your breath—and sleep
within this window of stars,
afloat and heavy, slow and clumsy
but feet dipped in this ocean, catching waves,
like butterflies, in the net of my dreams.

Morning Prayer

For my son, Himmat

A ripple beating, beating,
you arrive in a golden bough
the circle of love
a bangle of sky.
They stitch my womb after
the supple hold of amniotic fluid has let you go.
I am heavy yet, with unease
though the air is balloons
I am the first purple pansy, flushed
with the blood of spring.
The womb is a lair that remembers your smell
your whiff in my heart
you take root here.

When I start praying,
The wrath of the wind is in my mind.
I shut it out with the weight of a whale,
angst lodged in some inside cave,
and only I know its cloudy load,
I smell hunger like a lioness
pray with open eyes for God's grace—
the sun beams out silver rays
like meshes in the sky
but a leap of fear is fresh still, and soars

through this rusty door.
I believe in the dust-laden tree out yonder
in its needle leaves that don't let go
of the moist promise
and my butterfly kiss on its roots breeds.

These closed meditating eyes
belong to everyone.
Behind the lids is a secret
within the trunk is a trickle of gum.
Slow it moves;
soundless, I hear
till the promise in my heart
is under its feathers, hatching.

Storytelling

For my son, Himmat

I tell that story again—
The Arabian Nights throws an anchor
again, this time between us.
He looks for a genie in his lush head
which is not a lamp or a glass bottle;
outside, around the corner of our lawn is a tree
but only the vinegar smell of oranges
disturbs its magic bough,
this one cut like the Mad Hatter's hat of ruins.

He thinks soft as butter
and asks again "What is a genie?"
(I think it looks like a Roman bust in smoke)
I blow up a cloud of baby powder and light up
a rocket from a science book—it is something like this.
He says, "What colour is it? Does it look brown?"
I place a white daisy in an ink bottle and wait.
A colour collects in the petals.
He beams, "Is a genie blue? Is he like Krishna?"
More like the poison lodged in Shiva's translucent throat.
"Is he a god?"
No, and I pick up *The Illustrated Life Stories of the Gurus*
and try to arrive at a story to tell him.
He points to the one about
Guru Nanak and the pundits at Varanasi, and
I act it out for him
and conclude with a moral, God is everywhere,
so you can pray anywhere and any time.
He says, "How do I pray?

I want to explain to him these lines from *Kirtan Sohila:*[2]
Upon that cosmic plate of the sky,
the sun and the moon are the lamps,
the stars and their orbs are the studded pearls,
the fragrance of sandalwood in the air is the temple incense,
and the wind is the fan.
All the plants of the world are
the altar flowers offered to You, O Luminous Lord.
What a beautiful Aartee, lamp-lit worship this is!
O Destroyer of Fear, this is your Ceremony of Light.
The Unstruck Sound-current of the Shabad is
the vibration of the temple drums.
These—their music passed to me by my mother—
I chant and he sleeps.
I chant and cannot sleep.

---

2   *Kirtan Sohila* is a night-time prayer of the Sikhs. It comprises verses written by three Sikh Gurus, Guru Nanak, Guru Ram Das, and Guru Arjan Dev. This translation is taken from: Singh, Sahib. *Nitnem Satik.* Amritsar: Singh Brothers Publishers, 2015.

The Star Within

It is energy, burning breath, sparkle film
a thin spark that holds the tug of fire in its heart,
clots of grinding glow at its edge.
It has litmus core, osmotic tissue,
transpiring pores that ooze heat.
It beats in its silent universal drone
it explodes flowers in the heart,
how beautiful its lives,
diaphanous, bouncy, ventilated,
how you yearn for it when it dims
leaving trails like a brush.
You search its footsteps to reach its lair;
its smell mesmerizing,
its poppy seeds exhilarating, spruce up the mind tree,
its roots dip here, in the kernel of dreams,
flames rise to it in wishes
snuggling clouds are not its sinister end.
This star that sometimes seems dying
these cracks in Venus that dare
it crumbles, has debris, foggy breath—dusted and soft
it flounders, stammers—ruffled and tired
it burns, cauterized breath walking this alley and
it sings of light in the darkest of nights.

Sati

I stumble over their stringent promise of death
this pyre, a casement
of perfume they dip me in.
How it sticks to my lips.
And death's ligament peels in places
when they plug it with fire.
I'm already a turnip,
how I melt into the air.
My shrieks
forced out of a thorny throat.
This is how I take flight—through
the blisters of my final roast.
The veins burst
I'm become the sun with fading rays
I melt before I can see his face
I melt with my vows, I am wax
already dripping when the worshippers see god.
This is what it takes to become a goddess
while the priest, is comfortable being a man
in the sultry nooks of his mind.

On a Photograph in a Social Studies Textbook

It was from long, long ago,
windy desert wrenching the soul.
In the coils of its henna designs,
huddled they stand,
women stiff under a tree,
a trail of earthen pots lined up
like the many abdomens of a caterpillar,
The Thar Desert, severe, the wind gathering,
heavy stoles pulled over their faces,
I always wondered if they spoke to each other
in that moment in the desert storm
or were their worlds torn
away by the wind
and shredded to bits?

Years later, on an unsung day,
the stemma brings a story
a grandmother speaking to what
she thought was a phantom in the wind
a woman
under our veranda staircase
stranger become ghost.
My grandmother told her it was
a praying house with images of gods
and nothing would get her into it.
The woman replied something
but the wind ate it away
while from the lattice door
my grandmother, the landlady spoke fearlessly
her faith firm, another had
words carried away by the wind

blowing out of a sore throat
into the whirlpool of the cyclone.
Quietly she had vanished when the
next day my grandmother
opened the morning doors.
The memory of the evening already swept clean
from her praying mind.

Anthophilous

Then, I did not know what
kaleidoscopes waited in that hour.

The summer wait of the playful evening flushes
my cheeks in the sun,
I sit by the lattice door
too heavy to vanish into
the bubble of the setting afternoon;
these wilted days droop with
the sun's snuggle in their roots.
Gathered toys sit on wallpapered shelves.

Then I was living among flowers.

These pansies in the pot
with tiger feet
thin purple petals bunched
together, as though to survive the summer heat
but the sunny spot at their nape throbs.
It dries out last
it is smooth
it is where the petal, leaves, stalk, come together
it is where his hand tried to pluck me
before I could dry up enough and
float a seed into the womb of summer.
When he left me midway,
a petal was left
waiting for the smell of seed.
Curved towards the soil
its neck turned away from the sun
sorry for itself
unable to see.

Art Workshop in a Slum[3]

Those are days of the sun,
winds of loo, and a wait of rain,
and in the midst of this mountain,
a casement—a lonely lake of ripples.
Then they come

with their marbles and stones;
the air buoyant in their feathers
they think first—huddled together,
like a foggy morning—it is a drill.
They have doubts under the
stern sun that never forgets.

But then, every day after that,
a current cuts through,
the snow melts
the hands are trellises
and a mosaic forms from their
holy frescos
fire and sand are tilled in this wait
for water.
Last paintings are like boats
easily afloat in a lake
because the rain flushed-sky dips
its branches to climb
and the boats float through this straw stubble.
The air bloated, I can feel the rain
it's raining in the hills
I can feel it coming up under my feet
up my legs
and the surprised summer gapes.

3   This poem is based on the experience of teaching painting to the children
from the Daru Kutiya slum.

On a Map Reading

It was blistered in places, a debris magnet
dissolved in the hot damp of my sweat.
I scamper over it with knowing paws
I bring together the freckled plains for them to see.
This.
The Ganga Brahmaputra plain
the Himalayan surge here
the Aravali encampment there.
I make the monsoons with a sweep
I am a wind lunging up the Himalayas
precipitating, showering, crashing.
They said,
We did not know
what
India is like. On a map.
Or how rain is made.
But we know. They chanted.
We know. We are the Aravalis.
We run parallel to the winds.
We make the Thar Desert.
We are stone.
We knock at the earth.
We are the blood and tissue of its flames.
The plaid surface of the wind.
We collect. Dust.
We are the deposit. Of dreams.
A face. Singular to you. Quiet and seething.

A Poet on Baisakhi, 1919[4]

She is a poet and it is 1919.
The news of the massacre is raw as
winter wheat, just before
the gold steps in with fairy breath.
She writes epistles to a sky that
is now always a dark closed room,
she swims in its fabric, but today
the stars droop, eyes fixed
on the blood at their feet
the soil is coarse and clods
of shot-out bones are scattered in the grass.
When the clouds crack, she is
already offering blood-dried jaggery to them.
The inky fingertip is her offering to
the white sky. Even after it has happened—
this massacre—she is still praying,
"It should not happen."
The blood between her thighs
and her pen, are lost that same day
and the same day the river changes course
the fireflies hide in the sand by its banks.
It is three become one, pen-woman-river
they flow on the rugged terrain,
they fumble for sound
and then aflutter,
they rise in waves for the cleansing rain to wash away
the stray whiff of death.

---

4   Baisakhi is celebrated in Punjab in mid April on reaping the wheat crop.
In 1919, when India was still under British rule, hundreds of people gathered
peacefully in the Jallianwala Bagh to celebrate Baisakhi, and were ruthlessly
massacred by a British general.

The Splitting

(On India-Pakistan hatred)

These lamps, a glass mesh
what flames will they cradle?
This beam that slips,
what stones will it shove into the river?

This desertion
sandpapers our hearts and the
scars of the noose are fresh.
The loud promise becomes a murmur
the land markings—tissues nobody peels
the forest fire spreads.

If a dandelion flies from my heart
they burn it in flight
a corpse drips
they transfuse more blood,
every time a nerve in it twitches,
they pluck it out.
Old as a plateau it has the
nine lives of a cat;
we've lost count.

Maybe the corpse will turn on its side.
Maybe the dandelion seed
will land in his heart from across.
And the tide will come
before we too die.

For My Grandfather

I searched for you on the internet
hoping to find a family tree.
The world is shrunk to a village,
but this difference between us
is a meadow the size of the sky.
Here I wander plucking wild flowers
and you sit, a hawk
in the branches, looking at me.
Here I see the vanishing light
behind the moon's icy face,
and I head back home before
the evening can cast its shadows on me.
The days are sombre
and I burn wreaths of old time
for the firmament
to fly them to your chest.
I have lain in your pyre
but then you bend the branches
to shed over me their shade;
When I look into your gesture
the wind shows its direction
and the dust shifts.
I return at your altar day after day
you are still, but the silver
frames of my letters lay these
leaves at your footprints,
slivers of your tenderness.

Artist

She made me this bandaged ear
and then placed it
in a box she will bury today.
This blood she has already washed
between layers of the moonlit sky
till its seams are red at the city's horizons.

She made for me this whirl of stars and
the dripping milk rain. Someone squeezes in the sky,
the cow's udders,
and a bird opens its beak on a dry tree;
its tongue is a flame that shivers but
she opens this cavern to motherhood

She made me this smooth, slow breeze
that stumbles at sinew and bone
it sings love songs into his ears and
opens a sphere with its nimble fingers while smooth leaves
are pulled by her breath on harmonica strings.

Not Every Poem

Will have trellises of blood
climbing up it.
Sometimes the juice of love dries
and haphazard flaky leaves are
all that the hands
tear from this vein.

Sometimes words are a lake
you can bend to see
a reflection of your face,
it is quiet and never disturbed
by a reflection until a dove drops
a pebble on it, resurrecting a wall of ripples.

Sometimes events are rusty as a lock
without a key; this room shut to glows.
You cannot open the windows and
the air grows musty.
When you return with the key the next day
the air already feels different.

And this poem cannot drink the last
snuggle of word and thought.
They sit looking into the growing
distance between each other's eyes.

A Day with Keats

He had a hand both warm and clammy
I held its sun spots and dry icicles;
after all, writing about an urn sucks out
the sparks crackling in your deepest core.
He had a cough that never died but
he lit up a flame from his throat
the wick soiled by these momentous years

that was it, the urn of passion,
containing ash and bone
the crackling fire leaping out.
Was that the last light in the heifer's eyes?
I have seen this cold blood that stills like
a leaf on both sides of this pot
because I have withered
and then I meet you withering too.

It started with sparkling wine and the blue
mouth of an abundant autumn
and the Lethe had already
patched your face in me
but the sound goes last and the
nightingale speaks through the dark.

Then I know what a favourite poem is.
Rounded like a ball of ice in a Punjabi summer,
before you try to write it, it is already melting
and its sweet lingers.
It leaves streaks of colour on your tongue
it takes you to a Venetian stream
the gondola wobbles under our feet at first

and the oars are heavy but then
the fish of delight leap up.
We sit still in our boat and
a golden fish lands between us.

A Van Gogh Tale

Van Gogh's eyes opened up in the landscape
and fire flung itself from the mossy trees.
The first caw of spring
the bare chapters written in black
this fish line solitary in an icy pond
this tongue wringing itself dry—
how warm grow his eyes in the forest.
Now as I walk on it,
their warm breath on my hands
becoming brushes, then varnish, then
trees with stolen days.
This eye is a pothole pitted with seeds,
a squishy fruit shedding its cataract
nudging the frost of a quiet sun's light;
this froth by the pond of eyes
bubbles itself to oblivion,
these quiet days receiving rain
this bird dashing through a still forest
this frozen dream in cherry blossoms
the sunlit heart of flowers
the rima within peasant shoes
the pirouettes of light in the sky—
not ominous, cooked in a cauldron with
witch broth, but torrid, sweltering in
fish mouths, till the lake is sailing in magma
and no fishermen remain.
This Viking tale shed miles farther than the fisheries
to a pit where sounds drown into fire-lit flesh
to a copse in the inky wind
where a song plays but you hear it

not until it is acrylic ribbons flung from the sky
not until it no longer gropes but still
a shore with shingles washing up over
its compass of arms.

I Like That Kind of Home

These are beautiful,
the rolling plains ending
in twin lakes—two oceans of
leaf flutter and fish furrow.
Grass grows like a pelt
on my animal memory. They part
every time a bird lands between this chasm
to nestle on her eggs, and when
they hatch, the grass closes
over their yellow bodies
like the hands of a mother.

And this mountain with manicured
hands—it rolls down
a clod every now and then.
It scares me. I'm made for the Savannah.

The Savannah digs up a hole
in my mind and throws in a rustle.
I am relieved in its ancient promise
I drink it in, under sparse trees.
I am filled with this memory
scratching its back like a lioness
rolling in these cupped hands of the earth
I drink from this gesture
this posture that the grassland
has taken as it bends into me.

A Butterfly Sees

Butterflies may not have a human's sharp vision, but their eyes beat us in other ways. Their visual fields are larger, they're better at perceiving fast-moving objects, and they can distinguish ultraviolet and polarized light.
-Virginia Morell

Seams of colour
shine in a mist and the empyrean
stage shudders with flowers.
I do not see the blue of a petal
against the sky or
the darkening centres of
this garden that growls to her to come.
The flower is a dissection
of quivering colour in her eyes
and they are four bucketfuls
of colour and crayon.

And then, this colour game is the
conversation of pollen and moist feet.
An echo in some long cave.
And I in this repartee with a page, sit here
trying to understand a butterfly
when my mind is sore from
a scent going in and out of my historic brain.

Sea Otter

. . . the sea otter, a cat-sized cousin of weasels that lives along the coast from Alaska to southern California. Because its luxurious fur was so much prized, the species was hunted to near extinction by the end of the nineteenth century—with a catastrophic ecological result.
—Edward O Wilson

They snuggle, inside the wave
having hitched a ride, they crawl
slowly towards the horizon's net
and their faces twitch.
They send the sea nymph into a frothing fit.

This human world pulls in
everything, tornado and teeth
fibre and flesh, fresco and prayer.
Sifted on a darkening ocean, these creatures
saunter zombielike in the coils of the sea's belly.
The nymph becomes a witch
the ocean, an enzyme that grows sour.
An otter is pulled out of the sea's body
like a golden lung.

And the kelp forest slowly retreats under sea soil,
a desert of design— sometimes at night—
this jungle sends out
roots like little moth antlers
looking for a den.
The kelp splashes up a head, only to
hide under the sand again.
It awaits the hands of the sea otter
to pull up its dormant threads
and stitch them to the sea's promise.

Fire

The single-eyed furnace of life
this one that blasted itself into existence
burning space.
Vultures orbit it, bodies of the same beat.

Here the fire is a flower
the one that burns pyre and widow
this offering to fire, did it ever grow roots?
This chunk of flesh you burn, does it beat?
This flower you pluck from the pyre
and put it on a tray for the gods,
with coconut, rice, turmeric, vermillion—
if you want to talk to God, is this how
you present your offering?

Glow of light in the body
I can burn because it's in me,
fire quenches because everything is it.
It wants us all back
eye, scalp, heart
sinew, pulse, beat
till the fire, and a promise rises from it.
Douse it with water and it waits in ash.
Freed of body or base,
it can light up in midflight.
If space knew a letter it would be this.

Extra Terrestrial

She is a swimmer, parting
galactic oceans with feet and fin
land dweller, with a memory of water
dormant in her gills, flapping no more.

Like me, from the land's fluorescent ribs,
she extracts radiation and
pulls her world through its rings
an ocean of muslin, floated through a ribcage
these that grow piping hot
scalding hot, hot enough
to roll her civilizations
on for millenniums.

She is like me, she walks
quite sure of her two legs,
with the bulk of a thin bear
and pulpy paws extending
to hooked fingers.

Goblets set in her sockets
drink. Only her feasts are roomy
and the shrill of her voice
is silence to me.

You can dissect her
and see the pattern
of a sure flower in her abdomen.
With just these counted tendrils
and counted arteries of stamen.

She munches a different seed
like a parakeet she will not
survive here because
she smells another musk.
This food is different, but
her teeth set in her jaw are like mine.

This eye of hers can read me
and yet her laugh is different
a twitch in the eye is her smile
and it is not my happiness that she feels.

She lives in a chamber full of people
who hold hands and those
never really unclasp even when they wander away.

She buzzes a bee down my window
and through her eyes she reads my books
she walks slowly around my gods—
and they, rapt in *tandav.*
She encases my voice in a sound box
but never alights,
never calls, she is what I think, shy,
she sits composed in her corner
of the universe and sees
the difference superficial, between us.

Room

This room hasn't gathered dust
as I thought it would
the serene walls ooze marble breath
slated in the slime of rainy memories
but the air, lustrous and polished,
hangs about it as before.
The cupboards say
that I had left.
The clinging jargon on their doors,
drags old worlds through the mind
I can smell memories in the curtains

and the slow music playing
under darkened eyelids is different,
someone has arranged dead butterflies
on a wall. They look sinister
stuck corpses, gathering dust, dance.
A mirror is broken; almost,
it shows another face.
As broken calls broken,
a conversation trips through the cracks
falters and falls without an echo.
Soon the sun will set on it again
and ghosts will come alive in my lair
with their pillow talk and flushed
faces in the mirror
some lizard will stretch
invisible antlers behind the lamp
looking for food
she lives here, I am a visitor.

My old self
has surrendered its robes and walks
this pool naked. It plumbs the past.
When it scampers out, it is golden
while I who stand almost at
the doorway, am silver
I shiver in the light of the risen moon,
walk through my aura
I left in this room, that I could not lock.
But this flower has bloomed again
in between the pages of memory, its sap sticks
while silverfish run through this
roughly preserved flower.

Sinking

She floated on the ocean for an hour
it dipped into her and
its chill entered her bones.
Afloat, she was a sickle cutting the waves
till numbness invaded
her foreign figure.
The mind was the last to give
up to the ocean's lynching
its salt singing lullabies
into her ear. She waited for
the splash of the sun
and then the sea whispered
a death song and its stillness welcomed her.
That was when she gave up
to the sea's
immense weight
this ordeal became a dance in her mind
the brain became a bubble
what is it that colours the mind's depth?
But under the water she fights
the soul surrenders, the body wants to live.

Evolution

On "Girl at Window" by Salvador Dali

Before this glass was set in its frame,
the sea salt was already splashing and
its misty mouth had uttered a promise.
And then we came, weaved from a chain
and refracting light

But she hears only the aching, struggling footsteps.
All the time, she cleans this window,
someone stands by it and looks
into the scene. His eyes are black holes
they leave for her only
the jagged endings of this scene.

A woman looking into eternity
with a horizon beyond which some water
is a colour she has never seen.

Repression

The melanin
is still there under my nails
my eyeballs are the colour of the sky
my blood falls in clots between my legs

I think I have shed this ghost in
a quiet pyre of my accessories—
this molar crown
shaved hair from my armpits
and the bone they extracted long ago,
saying it was too long to lodge in me;
I burn these, but when
they pick my flowers
from the burnt out pyre
the bone is there,
ash-coated, marrow dry,
but white as a pearl,
in a dark oyster shell.
It refuses to die.

Neurotic

Hissing bed, and limbs light as a bat
he must hang here
under dead bridges
he wanders this
deserted turf and suicide bodies
in his closed heart rotten
with an apology in blood
that never reached God.

He strays from the sun like a sure burglar
his many faces etched in granite fetch fire
but he will freeze in the blizzard in his heart.
How vacantly this song affects others
walking the streets to work
but it is a nail in his head,
hammering, hammering till it's through.
The counsellors clamber around—
he is a museum wall. Here someone
points at a smear of blood
and he sees his hands, shiny and maroon,

here they have left their baggage
the sundry stones packed into a sack.
You spill them and they fall forever.
The ice, he cannot plunge,
the ocean will not hold his weight
and the rays speak through the open door
of fire, which melts the jagged corners of his sleep,
and he wakes up in
a world of the mildewed dead.

Normal or Abnormal

This starch test on
my heart is complete,
this pumping organ has given up its
eccentric ruffle with the wind.
Yet excited voices moan,
they uncurl in slow echoes
in the halls of these mountains.
The pine trees recoil in its tremor
but this uprooted bizarre
soul has taken root through
its cracked walls.
Shimmering leaves
crowd the sky.
Smooth assurances rise as
these leaves quieten in sunspots.

This abnormal trench where
the roots were once pulled out
has closed like a pair of praying hands.
They smoothen the soil with their notes
and I grow thick;
the trench sometimes
opens up, like a fresh wound, only to soon
coil like a burning snake.
This reality, I embrace.
That, I close shut in the attic,
still throbbing in its scars.

Sethe

On Toni Morrison's Beloved

She held herself as though
keeping the oddments of
her body from scattering
the cold that she tried to chasten,
rose to her eyes and whirled a tornado
from their punched-out wells of light
but the hammer goes
clank, clank.
This migraine beats under the
hoofs of this colt in her head
beloved is huddled in her heart
a storm curdles in its chambers.
Peep in and a man with a hat
is always riding
and the colt's hoofs go
clank, clank.
Thud, thud
on a heart of paper walls.
It takes fifty women to tame this one
it takes a whip and some magic
to wake up this ghost
to stop it shuddering.
How humid, her heart,
raining, raining
the clouds will rise
the mists will scatter
and she will let down her arms

let go of this body
but her hands
will be heavy
from the holding.

Fables

Curling, curling this thick
rope in a tiger's heart is an emotion
blood fire in his eyes, its smell
evaporates before we arrive.
This frown in the elephant's musky smell
the rabbit's leap, the tortoise calm
are a story, and stories are clay pots
with invisible lattices.
Something always escapes.

Sleeping Beauty

This is time come to a standstill.
How long will the sands pour in the hour glass?
This single prick is hard enough to
send Buddha into convulsions
it takes exactly one hundred revolutions
for the kiss to compel life
then the clocks begin again
the bustle resumes
and Buddha awakes;
with the kiss of eternity on his lips
this betrothal is juice
its flood cuts through cobwebs and ice
it nourishes life back into the forest;
the hardened roots that clutched
the soil, loosen, are aired
the dog hanging in midflight
meditating on his bone, jumps.
This plunge is into the pricked
drop of blood and this hunger is quenched after
the dance slows to a trickle from a dike.

Beauty and the Beast

He trembles, in her embrace, a train of words
quite derailed: the child of storm speaks
magic drains from his melanin fangs
into her sterile hands.
She holds him in her shuddering soul
she is become a ripple that huddles a ship
carrying his indigo and spice.

This one that lies dying is a façade
wears an indigo robe under his pelt,
the one consumed by the fairy with
the crooked nose and sniffing soul.
He dies in the embrace of beauty.
And then in the midst of music and lights
another is born.
Not from a womb but a spell
he bites his own umbilical cord
hides his wound under the tissue peel
of her dress and shoves the beast under it, and
out of existence. Beauty, he abducts
clings to her apron like a child
always seeking her consent.
Who controls whom, this native
of the forest, can he smell?
Beauty is his rheumatic muscle,
apoplectic like a drowned boat;
when she does say yes in the
control of his maneuvering mind
he cannot be the worthy prince
unless she looks away.
He is born in blind light

and deafening sound.
This breaks the spell,
and the crooked fairy gives up
to this fist clenching, unclenching
in his mind. Slow as a spider he crawls on
shaking knees, stiff from being dipped
in a golden book of meanings so long
he chants his spell-hued book confused
and walks the distance of the aisle
to be wed to Beauty.

On Death

When you hear this music of my trepidation
this thud against the face of the earth
the dusk is in your mouth, and you stand at
the window contemplating the morning
already the stiff shoulders of death
are drooping over your body;
when the body of God is cut in two
you discover the bilateral symmetry of a pomegranate,
without the usual black and white.
Then the ocean is a murmur of our hearts,
its seeds, the ocean's weight carried in a fist.
Death is the word we do not utter,
it lies unplumbed,
quiet as a shell in a greying ocean cavern;
it whistles back to no sonar,
it does not open its eyes yet
and yet every night its gloating moan
wakes us just before we sleep
as the temple winds sing lullabies
and the columns echo with chants.

Raj. Mala. Heer.

Everyday I pass that empty house
with the letters engraved in bold brick:
"Raj. Mala. Heer."
And I wonder how old they are now
and where they dwell.

The cottage once isolated,
idyllic, is now implanted among others,
already extending its roots,
no longer spruced, old with a story,
quiet with secrets.

It is some haven,
I want to believe, where Raj Mala and Heer
still dwell, separated by periods.
I wonder if Raj is now old
and Mala sits beside him in her rocking chair

and Heer, a young woman
caressing her tresses
a dream child, already hatched
in language of their desire
with soft open hands that can be held.

How many engravings fade away alone
how many second thoughts waver in the wind
and cull out valleys in life's geography—
this orogeny that divides
and these words floating like seeds waiting to descend.

These writing hands are hers.
It is Heer's tongue that licks
the inside of my cheek,
her fists that hold on to the trickle
of words between my fingers and palm
my stiff promises that resonate in hers.

Conversation of Continents

We don't fit like those forgotten
silver spoons in my grandmother's velvet box,
she sits in my yard to hand
me the zucchini from her garden.
I present my bitter gourd.
Odd languages we speak
the table cloth converses
with the table in a windy tongue
our limbs are supple, our chords broken
we embroider words on fingertips.
And then these notes fill the air
a cavity opens in a hidden rocky cave;
open sesame, we say and treasures await us.
I show her a photo album from
my childhood in India
she scans it with a wondrous smile,
we talk about Italian and Kashmir shawls,
the rain, and she waits a little longer
in my porch than she did yesterday.

When our scents mix as if in
the earth's armpit, we sweat
our fever from across continents.
The blue carpet of the sky—yours,
and my yellow pelt blow two
different faces in the wind.
The golden glow of the sky is
a lampshade. Our rains drip
different sorts of music,
our Buddhas bear different smiles,
how do I hold you when

we don't fit like those silver spoons?
We remain silent some time
but not tired of talk.
When I utter, you listen,
and when you show, I see.
This is where our ocean currents
mingle and fish come to life
far, far away from their fisheries.
We wake up to this consent
to the supple muscle of this ocean
holding our puny boats.

Some Ekphrastic Poems

On Picasso's "The Weeping Woman"

She sheds glass tears and the scent
of the shriveled petunia that's in her hat.
She shivers as an ant
army eats away her saccharine gums.
Anguished wet handkerchief
stiff with the starch of her tears
her wail, long and slow, like a wolf howl.

She lives in the effluvium of war
her gasps grow on its trellises
her bald bones are baking in violence.
It is a winter war wearing a coat.
When it marches into summer
it will eat us high and dry. This sledge riding on *loo*,
is already halfway to the flaming valley.

How I wish this tear would dip in the sun behind
and engulf its heat with a drop—
who is here to pick at the carcass of my visage, but me?
To bury it, a hole is already dug in my face.
The scratchy throat swells in a song,
the war whistles for my soul to come.

On Matisse's "Woman Before an Aquarium"

In the light of evening
just before twilight throws a spell
on dull cones on the table,

she waits,
waits perhaps in a memory
to fling herself on her shadow;
the listless eyes are
drawn over her soul
like a sheet.
They pulse in yesterday,
these eyes coated in fins and feathers,
pulled over her scaly slithering lives,
these that are awake as eagles and
blue as a restless sea;
while the fish are slow, golden,
yet like her muffled race.
Weighed down by dreams that plunge
like anchors.
By the aquarium, a dry handkerchief but
today, she will not cry.

Bloom

On "Young Girl with a Parasol" by Edward Cucuel

She dips her head into the light—
but the parasol concealing desire,
it clutches her senses.
Head aglow and hair on fire, she writes this line.
But in her head she has walked on icebergs in
slippers into which her days fit
like slack feet.
Her dress quite overwhelmed
drips with her concealed pain
it catches sunspots like fire
this vacant Havisham face,
no hand can paint it still.

If buds around burst into blossoms,
their stench too will be torn
like the face under this mask of muscle.
Only the leaves above dance with slow
rhythms of pain,
the gradual ground gives in to blossom,
the blossom to light, and the light waits
in her lap to move up to her face
weaving poems in her head.

Mother

On "Mother Children Painting" by Amrita Shergil

She looked and barely a tear drop
stopped in her jaundice eye;
her light welled up
in the face of her daughter.
She gives her colour and cloak
her teeth may quiver in the
patched cheek, but her hands are rough
with motherhood and bent
into the light. They have no shadows.
This tattered hand is threads of pulse
she has been quiet a long time
her heart races but nothing scatters;
she can sniff a hostile brow
but waits.
She speaks in stories to her children
her mouth is quiet but not
the whimper they think it is.
It is as sure of words as her hand
that holds, and this that has welled up
in her is the strength of the light
she pours into her children
while she exists in their shadows.

Lilies in the Grave

A brain scan

I have somewhere a dried lily in the head.
I wish upon the scan,
the buckled ball of snow
daubed with orange and green,
I look closely, and there is yellow and blue too.

And then this shower of hail in my skull
the bruises—flowers shedding pigment,
ice lodged in cerebral cavities—

drooping on a summer stem
there is a hot fruit of fire.
Lucifer flocking souls in his bag
of snakes, the venom sweet
but they writhe through my nerves.
Forget the codeword and you are lost.
What seed was it?
Not sesame.
(You make its oil, and paint.)
Then slimy fingers become
snake stubs, foaming snakes.

Who let me out of this cave,
and flung the key into a Xanadu lake?
The hot copper sea at a mile
and the domes of ice,
the pines and mad haunting faces
make its molten paint.

The soil, stubborn,
the seas unarmed and I
forget where I buried the ores
but their hearts keep thudding.
I can hear them in the cracks in the uproar.
But what is this hammering,
this terrible fist in my heart,
this immersing anchor,
o' wayward leaves settle on this grave
leave the florets here.
Memories are brutal,
their scent faint, swells.
Somewhere in the heart.
It threatens to pour.

Haikus

Smooth sunshine stalks
extend to the sky's prism
discussing light

Banter of morning leaves
dies down when the noon's fingers
caress their pigment

Fireflies are aflutter
yet the night has dragged on
into the morning's wicks

Crawling comes the noon
opening the day's fist
on a gleaming toadstool

Clouds cluster thin
over moonlit skies
before they sail away

Can the sunspot absorb rain?
This pitter-patter disturbs
its talk with the earth

Flying kites are windy
they float in the sky like the smell of spring
on a new marigold

Rampant rain is dry today
the frogs finally sleep
the crows have wet beaks.

A Tree's Polychromasia

This fig rooted in collapsing mud,
it is a minefield of leaf and nest, snuggle of blossom
rootload after seething rootload of nerve,
singing to the water gods;
stem after stem of osmotic tissue, peeling in places
unperturbed onion selves; clustered foliage of
cloven branches falling to the sky.
We stand under it for a truce with the sun
we engulf the morsels of its shade
we sleep in the vacuity of its consent
interlacing ourselves with the winds in its skeleton.
This cupola of trees inflating the crag
shed the trauma of desire with their paralysis
this is where the wind gets its scent—
fluttering desire, sickle wave and rugged growl.
It's the beginning of marvel nests and Easter promises,
without eyes or face, the twin biform
of other trees seen in white light, not yet split
into spectrum and sense. It capitulates to Cuscuta and Viscum;
   it is
with thorny hands and needle leaves, but it does not give up
crescent and sunny promises made to the one in its boughs
and to itself.

Before Nirvana

You start walking to it and it,
the sun is still just a circle in the sky's lump.
Fanatic birds from Paradise whistle past,
winged furies that smoulder songs
vanishing from between their beaks
into silent strokes of an inner wind.
In their beaks is a glisten of gloom,
in their stride,
the seeds of a starry night,
and then in the gathering dark, a stillness,
the noise of feather dreams,
the slushy floods of fear,
and betwixt their two divided brains
the sun's promising palm, cut into a sphere.
Its vast expanse stretching wobbly fingers
as on a child's painting,
a poignant echo falls
into our senses if we look up to it.
This is a stiff load stretching on
the dial of this watch, the rumination
on a cliff, then the dip into smiling seas
and a grime-infested limb crumbling into heavy seas,
now clear, now catching the light,
now floating in the robes of a reunion,
learning both thunder and light,
heaviness and losing kinesthesia of touch.

The blazing swarm of fish trickles past
floating in their dance,
moving past the din of the day
into a smooth night of caresses.

This is a stay, not a story,
an emblem forever present where
the sky and ocean melt into one another,
this body is shed from the eyes;
feet, fins and feathers
all collect into an amphibian caress.

Morning

A whiff of monsoon is already in the air
when we pick up a brick, two beetles
crawl out with languid words,
the speech of frog croak is fleshy in the
brimming mouths of ponds
when the first eyes open to your face,
the night is already past, but the moon
refuses to rest. It is stuck on a bleached rampike
but silhouettes of the dark rise.
This daybreak becomes a cluster of breaths
that always return to wakeful eyes.

Acknowledgements

Guramrit and Himmat, this book has grown in your summery shades and winter's sunspots. The solace and cheer you bring to my life is immense; and even though I feel that most things can be contained, your love keeps overflowing into my life.

I bring forth this book in the memory of my late father-in-law, who will not be here to see it, but I'm happy I've read out parts of it to him. Your last words will keep me going for a long time to come.

I thank my parents for the wonder they led me to, and my brother for sharing my early days that seem the most natural; their enigma seems fading but their sound will resonate in me forever.

I thank the journals, *The Lindenwood Review, Phantom Drift Magazine, Zymbol Magazine, Nether, Pantheon, Cleaver Magazine, Taj Mahal Review, Dali's Love Child, Boschcombe Revoution, Pilgrimage, The Voices Project, Straylight,* and *South Asian Ensemble,* and the anthologies *Dance of the Peacock* and *All We Can Hold* for publishing my poetry.

-MKB